THE GOD IN YOU BIBLE STUDY SERIES

ALIVE!

GOD IN INTIMATE RELATIONSHIP WITH YOU

A Bible Study by

Churches Alive!

MINISTERING TO THE CHURCHES OF THE WORLD
Box 3800, San Bernardino, California 92413

Published by

NAVPRESS ▲ ®

A MINISTRY OF THE NAVIGATORS
P.O. BOX 35001, COLORADO SPRINGS, COLORADO 80935

Eighth printing, 1991

Cover illustration: Don Weller

Printed in the United States of America

Contents

Because we share kindred aims for helping local churches fulfill Christ's Great Commission to "go and make disciples," NavPress and Churches Alive have joined efforts on certain strategic publishing projects that are intended to bring effective disciplemaking resources into the service of the local church.

For more than a decade, Churches Alive has teamed up with churches of all denominations to establish vigorous disciplemaking ministries. At the same time, NavPress has focused on publishing Bible studies, books, and other resources that have grown out of The Navigators' 50 years of disciplemaking experience.

Now, together, we're working to offer special products like this one that are designed to stimulate a deeper, more fruitful commitment to Christ in the local gatherings of His Church.

The God in You Bible Study Series *was written by Russ Korth, Ron Wormser, Jr., and Ron Wormser, Sr. of Churches Alive. Many individuals from both Churches Alive and NavPress contributed greatly in bringing this project to publication.*

About the Author

In your hand you have just one item of a *wide range* of discipling helps, authored and developed by Churches Alive with *one overall, church-centered, biblical concept* in mind: GROWING BY DISCIPLING!

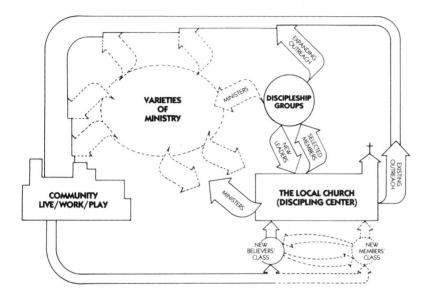

Convinced that the local church is the heart of God's plan for the world, a number of Christian leaders joined in 1973 to form Churches Alive. They saw the need for someone to work hand-in-hand with local churches to help them develop fruitful discipleship ministries.

Today, the ministry of Churches Alive has grown to include personal consulting assistance to church leaders, a variety of discipleship books and materials, and training conferences for clergy and laypeople. These methods and materials have proven effective in churches large and small of over 45 denominations.

From their commitment and experience in church ministry, Churches Alive developed the Growing by Discipling plan to help you

- minister to people at their levels of maturity.
- equip people for ministry.
- generate mature leaders.
- perpetuate quality.
- balance growth and outreach.

Every part of Growing by Discipling works together in harmony to meet the diverse needs of people—from veteran church members to the newly awakened in Christ. This discipling approach allows you to integrate present fruitful ministries and create additional ones through the new leaders you develop.

This concept follows Christ's disciplemaking example by helping you to meet people at their points of need. Then, you help them build their dependence on God so they experience His love and power. Finally, you equip them to reach out to others in a loving, effective, and balanced ministry of evangelism and helping hands.

Headquartered in San Bernardino, California, with staff across the United States and in Europe, Churches Alive continues to expand its ministry in North America and overseas.

Introduction

Jesus Christ made God in you possible. When you came to Christ, you became alive because God established intimate contact with you. In *Alive*, you will examine this intimate contact with God. You will learn the meaning, benefits, and responsibilities of God in you.

A good way to record what you learn is to keep a spiritual journal. You can begin your journal in this book, on page 61. Each week, record what you learn that helps you understand your relationship with God, a benefit from this relationship, and your responsibility.

Don't try to record everything you learn. Limit yourself to recording one highlight important to you. Some weeks you may not write something in every column. The important thing is to record what *you* are experiencing in your relationship with God. When you are through with this book, your journal may look similar to the example on page 9.

HOW TO USE THIS BIBLE STUDY. This book leads you through a unique approach to making the Bible meaningful. In each chapter you will study one passage, not isolated verses, to explore some of the major themes of God's Word. In the process, you'll learn Bible study methods that will be useful for the rest of your life.

You will gain maximum benefit from this book by completing the questions about the study passage and then meeting with a group of people to discuss what you discovered in your study.

No doubt, your group could spend many weeks exploring the richness of just one of these Bible passages. But much greater profit accompanies a pace of one chapter each week. This stride guarantees sustained enthusiasm that will leave people wanting more.

The leader's guide designed for this series aids the group leader in launching and guiding the discussion. It provides help for using the series in a home-study group or a classroom setting.

HINTS TO ENHANCE YOUR EXPERIENCE. The translation used in writing this study is the *New International Version* (NIV) of the Bible. All quotations are from this translation.

Though written using the NIV, this workbook adapts readily to other Bible translations. In fact, it adds interest and variety in group discussions when people use different translations.

Your book includes space to answer each question. But some people choose to mark some of their answers in an inexpensive Bible. Creating a study Bible like this allows a person to benefit from notes and information year after year.

Above all, *use* the insight you gain. The truths of the Bible were not recorded to rest on dusty shelves. God designed them to live in the experiences of people. In preparing this series, the authors never intended merely to increase your intellectual knowledge of the Bible—but to help you put into action the tremendous resources available in Jesus Christ.

JOURNAL

Passage	The Meaning of Being in Intimate Relationship with God	The Benefits I Enjoy	My Responsibilities
2 Corinthians 5:11-21	I have His righteousness	A new start	Be His Ambassador
1 John 1:1-10	We fellowship with each other	Light	Confess my sins
Romans 8:5-17	He lives in me	Life and peace	Live by the Spirit
Colossians 2:6-17	I mature in our relationship	Fullness	Continually live in Him
Hebrews 4:12-16	I can boldly enter His presence	Mercy and grace	Depend on Him
John 16:5-15	He is my Counselor	Guidance into truth	Obey His Guidelines
Psalm 27	He is my Companion	Goodness	Dwell with Him
Romans 8:28-39	I am never separated from His love	Total Triumph	Love Him
Psalm 19:7-11	He communicates with me	Continual revitalization	Be in the Word
Matthew 6:5-15	He is my Father	Answered prayer	Pray
Psalm 37:1-11	He champions my cause	Gaining my desires	Trust Him
John 15:1-17	I am a branch	Life Sustenance	Remain in Him

"Have you noticed anything different about Wilbur lately?"

1. Giving New Life

Study passage   2 Corinthians 5:11-21

Focus   2 Corinthians 5:17: Therefore, if anyone is in Christ, he is a new creation; the old has gone, the new has come!

---

1 The study passage states that when you first believed the gospel, you became a new creation, with several new possessions and a new position. Write several things the passage says are new about you.

Choose one of the things you listed on page 10 and explain why it is meaningful to you.

---

2 One of the words used several times in this passage to describe your new relationship to God is *reconciliation*. It is important to have a precise definition of repeated words to gain an accurate understanding of the passage. Using a dictionary, define *reconciliation* (or the verb *reconcile*).

---

3 The dictionary you consulted probably included definitions for reconciliation in relationships. How does being reconciled to God affect the following relationships? (You do not need to restrict your answers to these verses.)

You and Jesus Christ (Verses 15-16)

Your "new self" and your "old self" (Verses 15,17)

You and God (Verse 19)

You and others (Verse 20)

---

4 Your new life in Christ and your reconciliation to God are provided through the exchange described in verse 21. In the diagram below, write words or phrases that explain the exchange that has taken place.

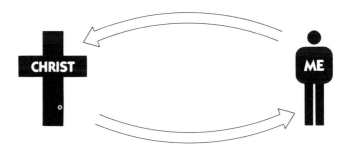

As you think of this exchange, how does it affect your attitude about yourself?

5 With your new life comes a new position. Verse 20 states that you are an ambassador for Christ. Use ideas you find as you reread the entire passage to explain what you think being an ambassador for Christ means.

**Ambassador to
the world,
representing
the Lord Jesus Christ**

(your name)

2. Lighting Your Way

Study passage   1 John 1:1-10

Focus   1 John 1:7: But if we walk in the light, as he is in the light, we have fellowship with one another, and the blood of Jesus, his Son, purifies us from all sin.

---

1 One of the main themes of this passage is fellowship—with God and with other believers. Use a dictionary to define *fellowship.*

What does this passage say about fellowship?

2 Repeated concepts almost always relate to the central theme(s) of a passage. For example, the concept of what we say is repeated seven times in this passage:

Verse 3—we proclaim
Verse 4—we write
Verse 5—we declare
Verse 6—if we claim
Verse 8—if we claim
Verse 9—if we confess
Verse 10—if we claim

Read these verses, looking for ideas on how *what you say* relates to fellowship with God.

How does what you say affect your fellowship with God?	How does your fellowship with God affect what you say?

3 Verse 5 states, "God is light." Though it is difficult to define, everyone knows something about light. From your experience and knowledge, list some facts about light.

What light does for me

Enables me to see.

How light affects my feelings

Choose one idea you wrote above or on page 15 and substitute it for the word *light* in the statement, "God is light." (For example, "God enables me to see.") Then give a brief explanation of what this new statement means to you.

4 Since God is light, a person not in fellowship with God is in darkness. Imagine you are walking down a pitch black alley. Without writing down answers, how do you feel? What are you thinking about? Now imagine you are given a flashlight. Where do you shine it? Why?

Record any insights this exercise gives you about the statement, "God is light."

5 According to the study passage, with whom can you have fellowship when you walk in light?

If you are walking in the light, do you think you can have fellowship with someone who is not walking in the light? Explain.

6 The local church is the main avenue of fellowship for most Christians. Using the concepts in 1 John 1, evaluate one of the following ideas (or your own idea) for improving fellowship. First explain why it might improve the quality of fellowship. Then tell why it might not.

A. Have coffee available at adult Sunday school.
B. Include time for testimonies as part of the worship service.
C. Conduct more social events.

D. _____ (your idea)

Might improve fellowship	Might not improve fellowship

My conclusion

Thinking of all you have learned in this chapter,
what does it mean to walk in the light?

From your understanding of the Bible and your own experience,
what do you have to do to continually walk in the light?

3. Residing in You

Study passage   Romans 8:5-17

Focus   Romans 8:9: You, however, are controlled not by the sinful nature but by the Spirit, if the Spirit of God lives in you. And if anyone does not have the Spirit of Christ, he does not belong to Christ.

---

1 Several times in this passage two opposite ideas, such as life and death, appear together. In the same way an artist uses light and dark colors, these opposite ideas provide contrast to emphasize important points. Find at least one pair of opposites in each verse listed on page 19. (Some pairs may be repeated.)

Verse 5   *Sinful nature desires / Spirit desires*

Verse 6

Verse 9

Verse 10

Verse 13

Verse 15

Verse 17

2 One pair of opposites mentioned several times is Spirit and sinful nature (flesh). Refer to the passage and identify concepts associated with the Spirit and concepts associated with the sinful nature.

The Spirit	The sinful nature

3 This passage provides a key to proper living: you must have a proper view of yourself. To live the way God intends, you need His evaluation, or view, of your life. What does the passage say is true about you?

Verse 9

Verse 10

Verse 12

Verse 15

(If there are other verses you think apply, list them, too.)

How do you think you could apply these truths to the following situation? You have to coordinate the planting of new rose bushes around the church building. At least eight other people indicated they would help plant the bushes on Saturday at 8:00 a.m. With this much help, the job should take less than an hour. However, at 8:00 a.m. Saturday, you are planting bushes alone. It takes you until almost 1:00 p.m. to finish.

4 A person controlled by the sinful nature cannot please God (verse 8). On the other hand, those controlled by the Spirit enjoy some wonderful results. What benefits mentioned in this passage give you the desire to be led by the Spirit?

What additional reasons do you have for wanting to be led by the Spirit?

What evidence can you find in the passage that God will provide the Spirit's control for those who want it?

5 The Spirit's control and the spiritual mind, referred to in verses 5 and 6, go hand in hand. What specific actions have helped you set your mind on the Spirit?

How do you think being spiritually-minded is exhibited when daily problems such as flat tires, forgotten appointments, slow traffic, and irritable children arise?

6 If you have asked the Spirit to lead you, but don't feel He is leading, what should you do?

Lord God, I trust You. And I believe what You have promised. Thank You for sending Your Holy Spirit. Live in me. Fill me full of Yourself. Cause me to recognize and respond to You.

4. Providing Fullness

Study passage Colossians 2:6-17

Focus Colossians 2:9-10: For in Christ all the fullness of the Deity lives in bodily form, and you have been given fullness in Christ, who is the head over every power and authority.

1 A newborn baby illustrates the difference between being complete (having fullness) and being mature. A baby is complete, having all the physical features of a mature person. As the baby grows, there will be no new bones or additional organs. But through growth, the newborn will develop the capacity to use what already exists.

In the same way, you are complete in Christ, yet need to grow. Using verses 6-8, identify characteristics of a growing

Christian. As you list these characteristics, also write down ways to develop or express them.

Characteristic of a growing Christian	Way to develop or express this characteristic

2 Your growth process is described in verse 6 as beginning when you receive Jesus Christ as Lord. Describe some of your attitudes and actions that were a part of your receiving Christ.

Verse 6 says, "Just as you received Christ Jesus as Lord, continue to live in him." Look over your description of the attitudes and actions involved in your receiving Christ. According to verse 6, these attitudes and actions are also how you are to continue to live in Christ.

3 Some people experience impaired growth because they fail to recognize or accept fullness. According to verses 9 and 10, what gives you assurance of your fullness (or completeness)?

4 Your fullness depends on the fullness of Jesus Christ. How is He presented in each of these verses:

Verse 6

Verse 9

Verse 15

5 Jesus has done many things that provide fullness for your life. What has He taken out of your life? (Verses 11,14)

What has He done for you? (Verses 12-13)

6 Verse 8 cautions against living according to philosophies that could imprison a Christian. One common philosophy in the world is, "If it feels good, do it." Identify another philosophy and explain how it can imprison people.

If people realize their completeness (fullness) is in Christ, do you think they are likely to be influenced by the philosophy you identified on page 26? Explain.

7 Your fullness is more than just an interesting idea; it affects the way you live. Read through the study passage and list the commands concerning how you are to live.

Choose one command and explain how obeying it *comes from* or *contributes to* your fullness in Christ.

All the fullness of Deity lives in Christ, who lives in you.
the Apostle Paul
Colossians 2:9-10
a paraphrase

5. Granting You Access

Study passage   Hebrews 4:12-16

Focus   Hebrews 4:16: Let us then approach the throne of grace with confidence, so that we may receive mercy and find grace to help us in our time of need.

---

1 Determine a main thought for each verse in the study passage. Seeing the main point of each verse helps you identify the theme of a Bible passage. A verse may present several thoughts, so choose the idea that is most important to you.

Verse 12   The Word is effective.

Verse 13

Verse 14

Verse 15

Verse 16

---

2 In verses 14 and 15, Jesus Christ is called your High Priest. Under the old covenant, the high priest was the most important person in the Jewish religion. He not only performed the same duties as other priests, but also was the one consulted when important decisions were to be made. Once a year, he alone could enter the Holy of Holies to perform special rites of worship before God.

Imagine you are living in Old Testament times and the high priest is coming to your house for dinner. How do you feel? How are you preparing?

According to verses 14 and 15, what is the difference between your High Priest and the Old Testament high priest?

What characteristics of your High Priest, as presented in the study passage, encourage you to approach God's throne?

3 Do you find temptation to be a barrier or a stimulus to approaching God's throne? Explain your answer.

If temptation makes you reluctant to approach God, what does the passage teach that can help you overcome your reluctance?

4 To help you apply this passage, list some of the temptations you experience.

5 There may be some temptations you were reluctant to list in the previous exercise. You may feel embarrassed, ashamed, or guilty about them. Why can you say that Jesus experienced the temptations you were reluctant to list?

How, then, do you think you should feel about yourself when you are tempted?

6 If you learned that a good friend of yours was tempted by something that also tempts you, how would you feel toward your friend?

What would you tell him or her?

7 One account of Jesus being tempted but not sinning is in Matthew 4:1-11. As you meditate on this passage, what do you learn from Jesus' example that can help you resist temptation?

8 If another person knew you in the way described in verses 12 and 13 of the study passage, what do you think his or her attitude toward you would be?

Do you think God's knowledge of you creates a barrier to approaching Him? Why or why not?

Praise be to God,
who has not rejected my prayer
or withheld his love from me!
The psalmist
Psalm 66:20

PORTLOK

6. Giving You Guidance

Study passage John 16:5-15

Focus John 16:13: But when he, the Spirit of truth, comes, he will guide you into all truth. He will not speak on his own; he will speak only what he hears, and he will tell you what is yet to come.

1 This passage contains only statements. There are no commands to obey and no history given. Jesus simply tells His disciples what will happen.

Write what you think is the main point of each verse. (Verses 9-11 are not included because they amplify verse 8.)

Verse 5   I'm going home.

Verse 6   You're sad.

Verse 7

Verse 8

Verse 12

Verse 13

Verse 14

Verse 15

Read your statements several times. What is the central idea that they communicate?

What title do you suggest for this passage?

2 There are two names for the Holy Spirit in this passage. What are they, and what do they imply to you?

Name	What it implies

3 The names Jesus used for the Holy Spirit reflect His character. Jesus also explained how the Spirit would relate to others. What action does He take toward

the world? (Verse 8)

you? (Verse 13)

Jesus Christ? (Verse 14)

4 Verses 9-11 explain verse 8 by giving reasons why the Holy Spirit convicts the world. From your experience, how do people respond to conviction by the Holy Spirit?

How do you think the Holy Spirit's convicting power should affect your communication with others?

5 This passage is part of a long talk by Jesus recorded in chapters 14, 15, and 16 of the Gospel of John. What additional information did Jesus give about the Holy Spirit in this talk?

John 14:16-17

John 14:25-26

6 Review the exercises you have completed, looking for statements about the Holy Spirit's guidance. Identify one area where you particularly desire the Holy Spirit's guidance right now.

☐ Major decision ☐ Marriage

☐ Finances ☐ Legal matter

☐ Children ☐ Other area: _____

What can you do to assure that you have the Holy Spirit's guidance in that area?

> In your unfailing love you will lead the people you
>   have redeemed.
> In your strength you will guide them to your holy
>   dwelling.
>
> Moses
> Exodus 15:13

"And then, Lord, I thought we'd go down and walk in the park . . ."

7. Being Your Companion

Study passage Psalm 27

Focus Psalm 27:8: My heart says of you, "Seek his face!" Your face, LORD, I will seek.

1 King David was known as a man after God's heart (1 Samuel 13:14). He wrote this psalm to express his feelings about his relationship to God and how enjoyable it was. What benefits do you receive from a close relationship with God? (Verses 1-3, 5-6)

2 One of the keys to maintaining a close relationship to God is having correct attitudes. Identify at least three attitudes David reveals in this psalm.

David's attitude	How this attitude is revealed
Vs. 1 - Confidence in God.	No fear of other people.

3 Close companionship always includes communication. David talked to God regularly. In your own words, list the things that David requested from God in this psalm.

Check two of the requests above that are particularly important to you right now. If you are able, list a promise from the Bible that indicates God will grant you your request.

4 In verse 4, David tells of his desire "to gaze upon the beauty of the LORD." Yet, Isaiah says about the Lord, "He had no beauty or majesty to attract us to him, nothing in his appearance that we should desire him" (Isaiah 53:2).

How would you describe the Lord's beauty, and how does it affect your relationship to Him?

5 David's close companionship with God gave him confidence in the Lord. What confidence did David express in verse 13?

What did this confidence enable him to do? (Verse 3)

6 What are some things David mentioned in this passage that often cause a person to experience fear?

What situation in your life causes you to fear?

How does David's example help you?

How does your relationship with God help you not to fear?

7 David concludes this psalm with a command—"Wait for the LORD." What do you think it means to wait for the Lord?

Why do you think it sometimes takes strength and courage to wait for the Lord?

---

8 Below are some factors listed in the psalm that contribute to developing a closer relationship with God. Identify an item in the list (or choose one of your own) that you would like to strengthen in your life.

_____ Desiring to know God (verse 4)

_____ Praying (verse 7)

_____ Accepting His mercy (verse 7)

_____ Seeking His face (verse 8)

_____ Following His guidance (verse 11)

_____ Having confidence in God (verse 13)

_____ Trusting Him (verse 14)

What steps will help you accomplish this?

O most merciful Redeemer, Friend, and Brother
May we know Thee more clearly
Love Thee more dearly,
Follow Thee more nearly:
Forever and ever.
                    St. Richard of Chichester

Armed to the teeth, Sunday school teacher Nat Willowby prepares
to do battle with the forces of darkness.

8. Assuring Your Triumph

Study passage   Romans 8:28-39

Focus   Romans 8:31: If God is for us, who can be against us?

1 Romans 8:28 says, "And we know that in all things God works for the good of those who love him." Give an example of how something that appeared to be bad for you turned out to be good for you.

Describe something in your life now that doesn't appear to be working for your good.

One goal for your study this week is to gain personal assurance that you are triumphing in this situation.

2 This study passage includes a long series of questions. Answering them will give you insight into God's care for you. In the chart below, list each verse that contains a question, write out the question, and then write your answer to that question.

Verse	Question	Your answer

3 You may have noticed that the phrase *all things* occurs several times in the passage. Use the chart below to record what *all things* refers to and what is stated concerning these things.

	What *all things* refers to	What is stated about *all things*
Verse 28		
Verse 32		
Verse 37		

4 The three statements in your chart above are positive, but at times, life has negative aspects. In your own words, tell how Paul describes his circumstances in verse 36.

Even when his circumstances were not pleasant, Paul considered himself to be a conqueror. What reasons for this attitude does he give in verses 37-39?

5 Paul lists several things that cannot separate you from God's love. Which of these things are most likely to threaten you personally?

6 When God makes a statement about your life, you can rely on it even though circumstances may seem to show that the opposite is true. In this sense, it is God's promise to you. Read the passage and, in your own words, write down what you consider to be God's promises to you.

7 One promise many Christians have claimed is in Romans 8:28. One paraphrase of that verse is, "God will cause all the hardship I endure to improve me because I love Him."

Look at the situation you described in question 1 that does not appear to be working for your good. How are the promises of Romans 8 assuring you of triumphing in this matter?

When Joseph's brothers saw that their father was dead, they said, "What if Joseph holds a grudge against us and pays us back for all the wrongs we did to him?" . . . But Joseph said to them, "Don't be afraid. Am I in the place of God? You intended to harm me, but God intended it for good to accomplish what is now being done."

Genesis 50:15-20

"Good . . . good. He's showing improvement."

9. Reviving by His Word

Study passage Psalm 19:7-11

Focus Psalm 19:7: The law of the LORD is perfect, reviving the soul.

1 The word *psalm* originally meant a twanging with the fingers. A psalm was written to be sung or recited while playing a stringed instrument. The Book of Psalms is a collection of these songs. They are a form of poetry in which you will often find rhythm and structure. In verses 7 and 8 one pattern is repeated four times: first, a *name for God's Word*; second, a *characteristic of God's Word*; third, a *benefit of God's Word*.

In the following chart, list all four names, characteristics, and benefits of God's Word given in verses 7 and 8.

Name	Characteristic	Benefit

Which benefit is most important to you right now? Why?

---

2 Considering the historical context of a passage helps you to understand and appreciate its meaning. In this psalm, David, the writer, compares God's Word to gold and honey. Imagine David, the shepherd, in the field with his flock, perhaps a little bored. Tell yourself a story that includes him finding a honeycomb. Try to see the events through his eyes. What insights did you gain from this exercise?

---

3 Psalm 19 is not the only psalm that records a person's response to God's Word. Psalm 119, the longest psalm, also centers on what God's Word means to the writer. Begin reading Psalm 119 until you find a verse that reflects how *you* feel about God's Word. Write the verse below, and briefly tell why it reflects your feelings.

4 To gain the benefits of God's Word, you must spend time in it. The chart below lists three ways you can learn God's Word. Fill in the columns based on your experience.

	Where I do this	What helps me do this	What I could do to improve
Listening			
Reading			
Studying			

5 Psalm 19:11 states that there is great reward for keeping God's Word. Next to each reference below, write the reward indicated. Then list any other rewards for keeping God's Word of which you are aware. Include Scripture references, if possible.

Psalm 1:2-3

Jeremiah 15:16

Matthew 7:24-27

Other rewards

6 The study passage promises several benefits of God's Word for your life. To experience these benefits right now, select a psalm, read it slowly and consider what it says. Be aware of the benefits you experience. Afterward, record your thoughts in the appropriate places below. (Don't feel pressured to have something written in every place.)

The psalm I read: _____ _____

It revived my soul.

It made me wise.

It gave me joy.

It enlightened me.

It warned me.

It _____

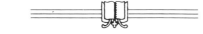

O come my people, to my law
Attentively give ear;
With willing heart and teachable
The words of wisdom hear.

My mouth shall speak in parables
Of hidden truths of old,
Which, handed down from age to age,
To us our fathers told.

We will not from their children hide
Jehovah's worthy praise,
But tell the greatness of His strength,
His wondrous works and ways.

Let children learn God's righteous ways
And on Him stay their heart,
That they may not forget His works;
Nor from His ways depart.

From Psalm 78
The Psalter

10. Responding to Your Prayers

Study passage   Matthew 6:5-15

Focus   Matthew 6:6: When you pray, go into your room, close the door and pray to your Father, who is unseen. Then your Father, who sees what is done in secret, will reward you.

1 Through His example and instruction, Jesus taught His followers things they should and shouldn't do as they prayed. List what Jesus taught concerning

things you should do when praying.

things you should not do when praying.

---

2 Prayer is talking with God. The more you know about Him, the better you will be able to communicate with Him. List the verses that refer to God in this passage. What does each verse reveal about God?

Verse	What is revealed about God

---

3 Jesus was one with God and knew how to communicate with Him in prayer. Jesus gave a prayer to use as an example of how you should pray. The phrases below and on the next page represent the "body" of Christ's prayer. Next to each phrase, write how you would express the same thought.

Jesus' words	My words
Hallowed be your name,	
Your kingdom come,	

Jesus' words	My words
Your will be done on earth as it is in heaven.	
Give us today our daily bread.	
Forgive us our debts, as we also have forgiven our debtors.	
And lead us not into temptation, but deliver us from the evil one.	

4 What part of His prayer did Jesus underscore in verses 14 and 15?

How does Jesus' statement in verses 14 and 15 apply to your prayer life?

5 Review your answers in this chapter and write a brief statement of what prayer means to you.

There is no way to learn to pray except by praying. No seasoned philosophy, by itself, ever taught a soul to pray.

J. Oswald Sanders
Spiritual Leadership

11. Meriting Your Trust

Study passage   Psalm 37:1-11

Focus   Psalm 37:3: Trust in the LORD and do good; dwell in the land and enjoy safe pasture.

---

1 God's commands are not designed to curtail your enjoyment of life. They are meant to enhance it. For example, when God says to forgive others, it is not because He has no interest in justice. He is interested in your harmony with other people and escaping the damaging effects of an unforgiving spirit.

List all the commands in the study passage that you think are part of trusting God. Also record the results promised. (Not all the commands have promised results.)

Command to trust	Promised result

Which promised result is most important to you? Why?

2 Many of the commands in this passage concern your attitudes. How do you think right attitudes help you trust the Lord?

How do you think trusting the Lord helps you have right attitudes?

3 Trusting in one thing usually means not relying on something else. According to Proverbs 3:5-6, when you are trusting in the Lord, what will you not be doing?

Describe a situation in which you obeyed Proverbs 3:5-6. What was the result?

4 Some of the commands of Psalm 37 are listed in the chart below. Considering how these operate on a human level can help you understand how to apply them in your relationship to God. From your experience, complete the chart.

Command	My experience in relating to another person	How this applies to my relationship with God
Trust.	I trusted Donna when I loaned her $10.	
Delight.		
Be still.		
Wait.		

5 It can be difficult to trust in God when you see people prosper who do not honor Him. What is your normal reaction when you see wicked people prospering?

Thoughtfully read verses 8-40 of Psalm 37. List three reasons why you are in a better situation than the wicked.

In light of these reasons, what do you think your attitude toward the wicked should be?

6 Apply the study to your life.

What is something you are tempted to fret about at this period in your life?

How do you know if you have quit trusting God and have started worrying about it?

How has this passage helped you? If it hasn't yet, how can this passage help you?

Even though my business deal falls through
and I don't get my expected raise,
though the bottom drops out of my stock
and all my investments fail,
though there is no money in the checkbook
and no food in the refrigerator,
yet I will rejoice in the Lord,
I will be joyful in God my Savior.
The Sovereign Lord is my strength;
He strengthens the fiber of my being and
enables me to rise above my circumstances.
                    Habakkuk 3:17-19
                        a paraphrase

"Quit worrying, Pitman. Every precaution has been. . ."

12. Sustaining Your Life

Study passage   John 15:1-17

Focus   John 15:5: I am the vine; you are the branches. If a man remains in me and I in him, he will bear much fruit; apart from me you can do nothing.

1 Writing a key word for each verse in a passage helps you identify important concepts and determine the focus of the passage. These key words can be taken directly from a verse, or they can be your own idea that captures the essence of a verse. For example, *vine* is a good key word for John 15:1. Verse 2 offers several good choices, such as *branch, fruit,* or *prune.*

Write a key word for each verse in this passage. When there are several possibilities, use a word that helps you recall the thrust of the verse.

Verse 1   Verse 9

Verse 2   Verse 10

Verse 3   Verse 11

Verse 4   Verse 12

Verse 5   Verse 13

Verse 6   Verse 14

Verse 7   Verse 15

Verse 8

Read over your key words and see how much of the passage comes to mind.

---

2 In this passage, Jesus used the example (analogy) of a grape-vine to help explain His relationship to you. In what sense does a branch *remain* in the vine? (Using a dictionary may help.)

What do you think it means to "remain in Christ"?

According to the passage, what is true of a person who remains in Christ?

Do you think a person can remain in Christ and yet not experience what you wrote on page 57? Explain your answer.

According to the passage, what is true of a person who does not remain in Christ?

3 Because they were familiar with vineyards, Jesus talked about a vine to help His disciples understand remaining in Him. Knowing about vines will help you understand this concept, also. Based on your knowledge or reference material, complete the chart.

	Natural vines	How this illustrates your relationship to Jesus
What is the difference between vine and branch?		
Why are branches pruned?		
How is fruit produced?		

4 List every clear statement about bearing fruit that you can find in this passage. Next, write the conclusion(s) you draw from these statements.

Statement about bearing fruit	My conclusion(s)

How should these conclusions affect your life?

5 It is clear from the passage that Jesus wants you to remain in Him. When you think about remaining in Christ, how do you feel? Complete at least one sentence below.

I feel confident because

I feel threatened because

I feel _____ because

6 Several actions are listed in the passage: remaining in Jesus' words, praying, obeying, loving others, and bearing fruit. How do these things help you remain in Christ?

How does remaining in Christ help you do these things?

At the beginning of this book, you were encouraged to keep a journal of the highlights from your study. If you have kept one, compare your journal entries to John 15:1-17. (If you haven't kept one, compare the sample journal on page 9 with John 15:1-17.)

Look for similarities between your journal and the study passage. One reason this passage was chosen to conclude this book is that it combines many of the ideas of the other study passages. It truly represents what it means to be alive in Jesus Christ by being in intimate relationship with Him. For example, being a pruned branch implies a new start (chapter 1). Remaining in Christ involves the concepts of fellowship with Him (chapter 2) and His living in you (chapter 3).

Continue looking for these kinds of similarities throughout the book by going through your journal. When you have finished, you will be able to recall many of these ideas anytime you remember, "I am the vine; you are the branches." Then you will be able to say, "I am *alive*. I am in intimate relationship with God."

JOURNAL

Passage	The Meaning of Being in Intimate Relationship with God	The Benefits I Enjoy	My Responsibilities
2 Corinthians 5:11-21			
1 John 1:1-10			
Romans 8:5-17			
Colossians 2:6-17			
Hebrews 4:12-16			
John 16:5-15			
Psalm 27			
Romans 8:28-39			
Psalm 19:7-11			
Matthew 6:5-15			
Psalm 37:1-11			
John 15:1-17			

Developing Lifelong Study Skills

The variety of methods you followed to complete the study are skills you can use throughout your life to understand and apply other passages in the Bible.

This summary identifies a few of the skills covered in this book, and will serve as a helpful guide for your future Bible study.

1. DEFINITIONS. Your understanding of any word is only as good as your definition. In Bible study you should attempt to work with the definition the writer had in mind. In chapter 1, you used a dictionary to confirm the definition of the word *reconciliation*. In addition to your regular dictionary, a Bible dictionary is a valuable aid.

2. REPETITION. Whenever a word, phrase, or concept is used several times, you have an important clue to what the writer considered primary. In chapter 2, you examined the repetition of the concept of speaking. Noticing the repeated use of a concept is more difficult than noticing the repeated use of a word. But finding repeated concepts will help you identify important teaching.

3. CONTRASTS. In art, dark and light colors are put in juxtaposition to emphasize one or the other. In writing, words with opposite meanings are used in a similar way. In chapter 3, you contrasted death with life and the Spirit with the sinful nature. These contrasts reveal an emphasis of the writer.

4. SIMILARITIES. We often learn about a new or strange topic by seeing how it is like a familiar subject. Bible writers made numerous uses of this technique. In chapter 4, you saw that your life in Christ is like receiving Him as your Lord (Colossians 2:6). Whenever you find the word *as* followed soon by the word *so*, look for similarities.

5. CROSS-REFERENCES. It has been said that the Bible is its own best commentary. Comparing one passage of Scripture with another will often clarify, amplify, or illustrate a concept. In chapter 5, Matthew 4:1-11 was used to illustrate Hebrews 4:15.

6. KEY WORDS. In chapter 12, you wrote a key word for each verse in the study passage. These key words formed a type of summary for the passage. Identifying one key word for each verse will help you review and learn a Bible passage.

OVERVIEW OF THE
God in You
SERIES

The book you hold in your hands is one of six in the *God in You Bible Study Series*. Each book complements the others as you explore the many privileges of God in you.

JESUS! God in You Made Possible

Immanuel	Luke 2:1-20
The Word	John 1:1-18
Savior	John 3:1-21
Friend of Sinners	John 4:4-26
Master	Matthew 8:23-9:8
Christ	Matthew 16:13-28
Servant	John 13:1-17
Bread of Life	Mark 14:12-42
Great High Priest	John 17
Man of Sorrows	John 19:16-30
Lord God Omnipotent	Luke 24
King of Kings	Acts 1:1-11

ALIVE! God in Intimate Relationship with You

Giving New Life	2 Corinthians 5:11-21
Lighting Your Way	1 John 1:1-10
Residing in You	Romans 8:5-17
Providing Fullness	Colossians 2:6-17
Granting You Access	Hebrews 4:12-16
Giving You Guidance	John 16:5-15
Being Your Companion	Psalm 27
Assuring Your Triumph	Romans 8:28-39
Reviving by His Word	Psalm 19:7-11
Responding to Your Prayers	Matthew 6:5-15
Meriting Your Trust	Psalm 37:1-11
Sustaining Your Life	John 15:1-17

RICH! God Meeting Your Deepest Needs

Love	1 John 4:7-21
Grace	Ephesians 2:1-10
Peace	Philippians 4:1-9
Acceptance	Luke 15:11-32
Clear Conscience	Hebrews 10:1-14
Wisdom	Proverbs 2
Comfort	2 Corinthians 1:3-11
Freedom	Galatians 5:1-18
Provision	Matthew 6:19-34
Family	Acts 2:41-47
Courage	Matthew 14:22-33
Hope	1 Thessalonians 4:13-5:11

POWERFUL! God Enabling You

CHANGED! Reflecting Your Love for God

FULFILLED! Enjoying God's Purpose for You

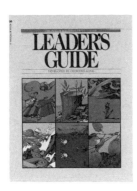

LEADER'S GUIDE

The *God in You Leader's Guide* gives help for every chapter in the series, including brief background information related to each Scripture passage, additional group discussion questions, and suggestions for the leader that will make the small group experience most helpful to the members.

FOR A FREE CATALOG OF
NAVPRESS BOOKS & BIBLE STUDIES,
CALL TOLL FREE 1-800-366-7788 (USA)
or 1-416-499-4615 (CANADA)